SCIENCE WITH AIR

W9-CFB-079

Helen Edom and Moira Butterfield

Designed by Sandy Wegener

Illustrated by Kate Davies

Consultant: Geoffrey Puplett

Contents

Air all around

Although you cannot see it, air is all around you. Try the experiments in this book to find out some of the things that air can do.

Things you need

The things you need for the experiments are easy to find. Here are some to collect.

Cartons

Plastic bottles

Bowl

Balloons

Straws

Being a scientist

Before you do an experiment, guess what will happen. Watch to see if you are right and write down what you find out.

Feeling air

How can you tell that air is all around you? Try flapping some cardboard next to your face.

The cardboard makes the air move. You can feel the air moving against your cheek.

The atmosphere

All around the earth there is a thick blanket of air called the atmosphere. Outside in space, above the atmosphere, there is no air at all.

A paper race

Moving air can push things around. You can use it to make this game work.

You need a piece of cardboard and a strip of paper for each player. Fold up one end of each strip.

You could add faces.

Fold here.

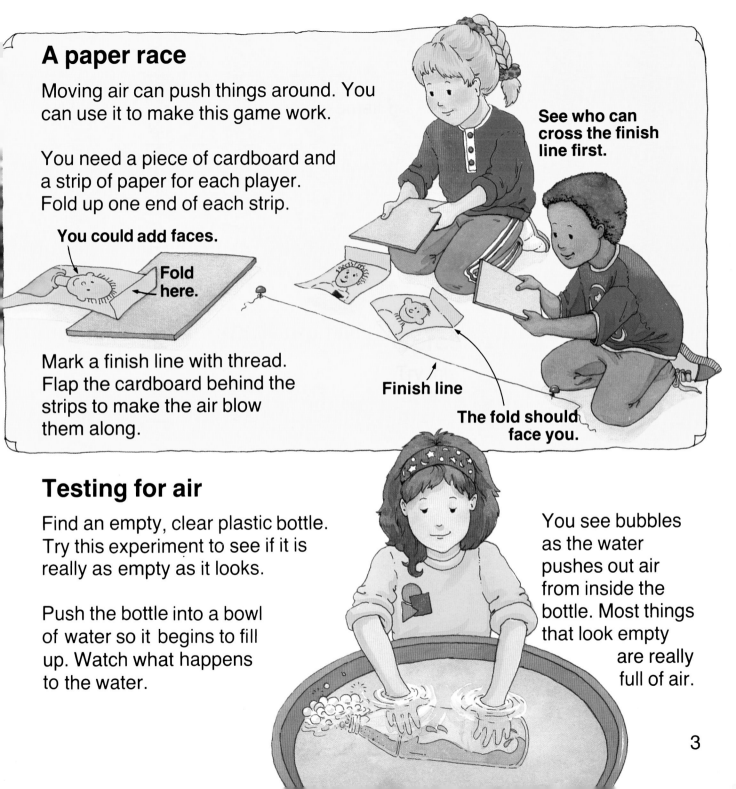

See who can cross the finish line first.

Mark a finish line with thread. Flap the cardboard behind the strips to make the air blow them along.

Finish line

The fold should face you.

Testing for air

Find an empty, clear plastic bottle. Try this experiment to see if it is really as empty as it looks.

Push the bottle into a bowl of water so it begins to fill up. Watch what happens to the water.

You see bubbles as the water pushes out air from inside the bottle. Most things that look empty are really full of air.

3

Air that pushes

Air pushes against things all the time. You are so used to it pushing against you that you do not notice it.

Heavy newspaper

Tear a sheet of newspaper in half and smooth it out on a table. Put a ruler under the paper so it sticks out over the edge of the table.

Use a new newspaper.

Stand to one side so the ruler cannot hit you.

Press down on the ruler to see if you can flick it off the table.

This is surprisingly hard to do because air presses down on the newspaper, keeping it in place.

4

Upside-down trick

This trick can be messy so try it over a bowl.

Fill a plastic cup full of water so the water bulges up above the top.

Put some cardboard on top and turn the cup upside-down, holding the cardboard in place.

Make sure there are no gaps between the cardboard and the cup.

Let go of the cardboard and see what happens.

Air pushes up on the cardboard and keeps it in place. This makes the water stay in the cup.

Collapsing carton

Sip all the drink out of a juice carton. Keep on sipping so you empty out the air. Watch what happens.

Use a cardboard carton with a hole for a straw.

When the carton is completely empty, the air outside pushes in the carton's sides.

Take the straw out of your mouth and watch the carton.

Air

The sides go out again because air rushes into the carton and pushes them out.

See what happens to the carton if you blow even more air into it.

Pumping up

Try pumping up a bicycle tire. Keep feeling the tire with your fingers to see how hard it is.

Air pushes harder when it is squeezed together. The more air you put inside the tire, the harder the tire feels.

Powerful tires

Air-filled tires are strong enough to take the weight of heavy trucks and tractors.

Changing size

When air gets warmer it expands, which means that it spreads out.

Disappearing dent

Watch what happens if you warm up the air inside a ping-pong ball.

Cover the glass, with a plate for example, to keep the ball down.

Watch the dent carefully.

First push a dent into the ball. Then put it in a glass full of warm water.

The water heats up the air in the ball, so the air expands. The expanding air pushes out the dent.

A jumping coin

You can use expanding air to make a coin jump.

Stand a long-necked bottle in a deep bowl. Wet the rim of the bottle and set a large coin on top. Then pour warm water into the bowl.

The coin must cover the hole completely.

Hold the bottle to keep it from falling over.

The warm water heats up the air inside the bottle. The air spreads out and pushes the coin upward.

Getting colder

Try this experiment to find out what happens when air becomes colder.

You could use an empty soda bottle.

First, put some ice-cubes into a plastic bag and crush them with a rolling pin. Then put the ice in a plastic bottle. Screw on the lid.

Shake the bottle, then put it down. Watch what happens to the bottle as the ice cools the air inside.

When air cools, it shrinks. The bottle's sides go inward so no empty space is left inside.

The cold air takes up less space.

Thunderstorms

In thunderstorms, lightning heats the air around it. The air expands so quickly that it makes a loud noise. You hear this noise as thunder.

7

Rising air

When air gets warmer it becomes lighter, so it moves upward.

Flying feather

Drop a small pillow feather above a warm radiator. See which way the feather floats.

Do not try this experiment above a fire.

The radiator heats up the air above it. The warm air rises and pushes up the feather.

Hot air balloons

Huge balloons can carry people underneath them. Burners heat the air in the balloon to make it rise. When the people want to land, they let the air cool again so the balloon sinks to the ground.

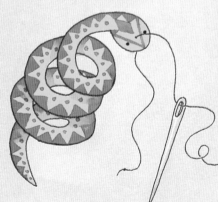

Wriggly snake

You can use warm air to make this snake wriggle.

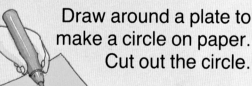

Use a needle to push a thread through the snake's head.

Draw around a plate to make a circle on paper. Cut out the circle.

Draw around and around inside the circle to make a spiral. Color the spiral like a snake, then cut it out.

Flowing air

In cold weather, go into a room with its heating on and close the door.

Hold a strip of tissue by the bottom of the door. See if the tissue moves.

Watch the end of the tissue strip.

The air in the heated room rises as it warms up. Colder air flows under the door to fill the space left by the rising air. This cold flow of air makes the tissue flutter.

Hang or hold the snake above a radiator.

The rising air makes the snake move.

Why there is wind

Wind happens because the Sun warms up parts of the land and sea. These warm parts heat up the air above them, like a radiator.

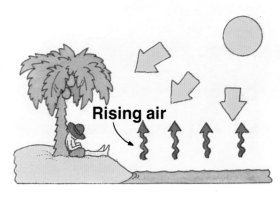

Rising air

The warm air rises and cold air flows into the space beneath. This flow of air is the wind.

Cold air

9

Wind

The wind is moving air. You can feel it push against you and see it blowing things around.

Strong and gentle

Look out for things that move in the wind.

A gentle wind, called a breeze, can make smoke drift, flags flutter and leaves rustle.

A very strong wind, called a gale, can make whole trees sway and branches break.

Dangerous winds

The strongest winds of all are called hurricanes. Hurricanes can travel at 320 kilometres per hour (200 mph) and blow away trees and buildings.

Changing wind

See if you can tell which way the wind is blowing. These tests will help.

Wet your finger and hold it up. It feels coldest on the side the wind is coming from.

Throw grass in the air and watch which way the wind blows it.

Try the tests at different times to see how often the wind changes direction.

Wind and rain

Look out for moving clouds in the sky. The wind moves clouds around from place to place, bringing the rain with them.

Make a weather vane

You can make a weather vane to help you find out where the wind comes from.

You need:
thick cardboard,
knitting needle,
cotton reel,*
sticky tape,**
scissors,
glue, pen,
clay.

Mark the directions, north, south, east and west on cardboard (see below).

Early in the morning, go outside and place the card so east points toward the Sun.*** Now all the directions are in the right place.

In the early morning, the Sun is always in the east.

Cut an arrow out of cardboard. Tape it to the cotton reel. Glue a circle of cardboard on top.

Make the tail large like this.

Put a blob of clay in the middle of the directions and push in the needle. point upward. Put the reel on top.

Use stones to keep the cardboard flat.

This arrow shows that the wind is coming from the north.

The arrow points in the direction the wind is coming from.

You could make a chart like this to show the direction and strength of the wind on different days.

Day	M	T	W
Direction	N		
Strength	weak		

Winds are named after the direction they blow from. For instance, a north wind blows from the north.

***Never look straight at the Sun as it can burn your eyes.

11

*Empty thread spool. **Cellophane tape.

Air power

You can use air to make things move. Try these ideas, then see if you can find any more ways to use air power.

Sailing boats

Float an empty plastic tub in some water. Try to blow it along.

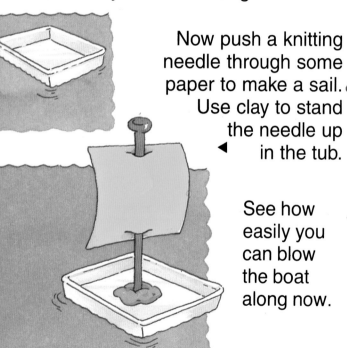

Now push a knitting needle through some paper to make a sail. Use clay to stand the needle up in the tub.

◀

See how easily you can blow the boat along now.

More air can push against the sail so the boat moves faster. Try different-sized sails to see which works best.

Rocket balloon

Air makes this balloon rocket along.

You need:
long piece of thread,
straw, long balloon,
sticky tape, peg.

Thread the string through the straw. Then tie it between two chairs.

Blow the balloon up and peg the end to keep the air from coming out. Tape the straw to the balloon.

Tape loosely.

Move the straw to the end of the string and take the peg off the balloon.

See how the balloon flattens as it speeds along.

The trapped air rushes out and makes the balloon move forward.

Windmills

Windmills were once used for grinding corn into flour. The wind turned sails to make machinery work inside.

Sail

Wind winch

This model winch can pull things up and down.

1. Trace the circle shape below on to cardboard. Cut out the middle. Then cut along the straight ◀ lines to make blades.

2. Bend each blade slightly. Then push the circle on to a straw. Hold it in place with clay. ▼

Trace this shape.

Bend all the blades the same way.

3. Use clay to stand the pegs up at the edge of a table, so you can fit the straw between them. Push the cocktail sticks through the pegs, into the straw.

Put the pegs upside-down.

4. Tie or stick a thread to the straw. Tie a button to the thread.

Blow here.

The thread hangs over the edge of the table.

5. Blow along the straw to make the winch wind up the thread. Put more buttons on to see how much your winch can lift at one time.

Moving through air

Some things travel through air better than others. Here you can find out why.

Paper puzzle

Tear two sheets of paper from the same pad. Screw one sheet up into a ball.

Both sheets are the same size.

Hold both pieces at the same height and drop them at the same time.

Can you guess which piece will land first?

Air pushes up on the paper pieces as they drop. The flat one is a bigger shape so more air can push against it. This makes it fall more slowly than the ball.

Pyramid pointer

Fold a square of paper in half from corner to corner. Open it and fold the other corners together.

◀ When you open the paper again you see four triangles.

Pinch one triangle in. ▶ Push its sides together so you can tape them.

Sides of triangle

Now drop the finished pyramid several times to see which way up it lands.

Try dropping the pyramid point-upward.

The pyramid always lands point first because the pointed end moves faster through the air than the wide end.

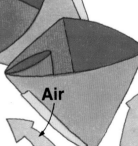

Air

14

Make a parachute

Parachutes are shaped so that lots of air can push against them.

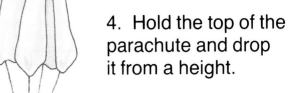

You need:
plastic bag,
scissors,
bucket, felt-
tipped pen,
sticky tape,
thread,
very light
toy, clay.

1. Put the bucket on the bag. Draw around it and cut the circle out.

◀ 2. Tape four pieces of long thread to the circle like this.

3. Tie the ends together and push the knot into the clay. Press the clay on to the toy.

4. Hold the top of the parachute and drop it from a height.

Watch how the parachute fills with air.

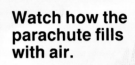

Air pushes up against the parachute so the toy falls slowly. Try this with slightly heavier toys. Do they fall any faster?

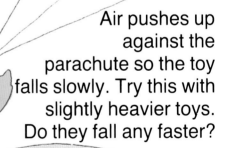

Go-faster shapes
Fast cars have smooth, pointed shapes. The air flows around these shapes instead of pushing against them. Shapes like this are called streamlined.

Flying

Planes can fly because of the way air pushes against them.

Make a glider

Fold a sheet of stiff paper lengthways. Then open the paper and fold two of the corners inward, as shown above.

Fold the new corners marked A down to the middle ◀ like this.

The corners meet in the middle.

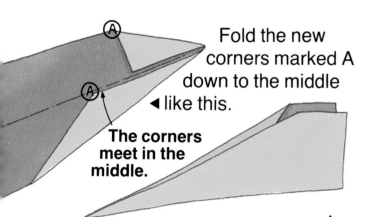

Fold both sides of the plane together with the folded corners inside.

Then fold the top edges down to make a wing on each side.

Fold the wings down one at a time.

Make a rudder by folding a small square of paper into a triangle.

Fold the corners together.

Glue the rudder between the wings at the back of the plane. Then cut slits to make one flap in the rudder and one on each wing.

Slits

Flying the glider

Try throwing the glider gently forward.

Air

Air pushes up against the wings so the glider flies a short distance.

16

Rising paper

Hold the edge of a sheet of paper just beneath your mouth. Blow across the top of the paper.

←—Blow hard.

The paper rises because the air beneath pushes harder than the fast-moving air above.

How planes fly

Faster air

Slower air

This shows a slice through the wing.

Planes have wings which are curved on top. When the plane moves, the air travels faster across the curved top.

The slower-moving air beneath pushes harder than the air above. This lifts the heavy plane up so it can fly.

Bend the rudder flap to ▶ the right. How does the plane fly now? What happens if you bend the flap to the left?

Bend this flap.

Bend these wing flaps.

Fly the plane with both wing flaps up and then down. Try again with one ◀ flap up and one down.

The air pushes against the flaps, making the glider turn, climb or dive.

How pilots steer

All planes have flaps on their wings and rudder. The pilot steers the plane by pressing levers which move these flaps.

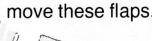

Breathing air

Your body needs air all the time. You get it by breathing in.

Counting breaths

For this experiment, ask a friend to time you with a watch that shows seconds.

Stand still and count the number of breaths you take in 30 seconds. Write this down.

Activity	Breaths per 30 secs
Standing still	10
Running	

You could make a chart like this.

Then run in place. Count your breaths again for 30 seconds. Is there a difference?

Your body uses part of the air you breathe in to help make energy. You need more energy when you run so you breathe faster.

18

Breathing bags

The air is made up of a mixture of gases. One of them is called oxygen. This is the part your body uses.

When you breathe in, you suck air into two spongy bags called lungs. They pass oxygen from the air into your body. You breathe out the rest of the air.

Your lungs are in your chest.

Oxygen travels in your blood.

Cleaning air

Your nose is full of tiny hairs. These trap dust from the air to keep you from breathing it in.

How much can you breathe?

Here is a way to measure how much air your lungs can hold. Get a friend to help you try it.

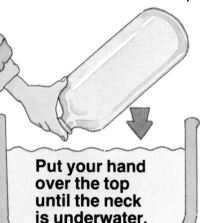

1. Fill a plastic bottle full of water and push it neck-down into a big bowl of water.

Put your hand over the top until the neck is underwater.

2. Turn the bottle upside-down, keeping the neck underwater. Push a flexible straw into the neck.

Be careful not to squash the straw.

3. Take a deep breath and blow gently down the straw.

The air goes to the top of the bottle.

One person holds the straw in place.

The space at the top of the bottle shows how much air you breathe out. Let your friend try this experiment. See who breathes out the most air.

Water in the air

Breathe on a window. Can you see or feel anything on the glass?

Does the glass feel wet?

There is water in the air. When air meets a cold surface, this water appears as tiny drops.

19

Sound and air

Try these experiments to find out how sound is made and how it travels through the air.

Shaking sound

Stretch an elastic band between your fingers and twang it to make a sound.

The band vibrates, which means it moves back and forth quickly. Sound is made when something vibrates.

See how the band moves.

How you make sound

Put your fingers on the lump in the middle of your throat and see what you can feel when you sing.

When you make a sound, parts in your throat vibrate. You can feel them shaking.

Sound-catcher

Smooth some newspaper over one end of a cardboard tube and tape it in place.

Sing through the tube and feel the paper at the same time.

The paper must be tight and flat.

Sing here.

Sound vibrations

The sound you make sends vibrations through the air in the tube. These make the paper shake.

Silent space

Out in space there is no noise because there is no air. Sound vibrations cannot travel through empty space.

20

Bottle music

Blow across the top of an empty bottle. See if you can make a sound.

When you blow across the top, you make the air vibrate inside the bottle. It makes a noise.

Put different amounts of water in the bottle. See if the sound changes.

The water pushes out some of the air.

The more water you put in, the less air there is left in the bottle. Smaller amounts of air vibrate more quickly and this makes a higher sound.

Musical pipes

Lots of musical instruments make sounds because air vibrates inside them. Here is one you can make.

Your breath makes air vibrate inside the straws.

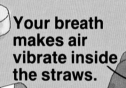

Cut some straws to different lengths. Starting with the shortest, lay them one by one on a piece of sticky tape.

Leave the longest straws till last.

Place another piece of sticky tape on top. Hold the row up and blow across each straw. See which makes the highest sound.

Notes for parents and teachers

These notes are intended to help answer questions that arise from the activities on earlier pages.

Air all around (pages 2-3)

Air like other gases, does not have a fixed shape. It spreads out to fill any available space so nothing is really empty. But air cannot escape from the atmosphere as the force of gravity keeps it from floating away from the Earth.

Air that pushes (pages 4-5)

Gases exert pressure in all directions. The pressure is affected by the amount of gas in a given space. When air is pumped into a tire, the valve keeps the air from escaping. As more and more air is pumped into the enclosed space, its pressure increases and it pushes strongly on the tire, keeping it inflated.

The trapped air pushes against the sides of the tire.

Changing size (pages 6-7)

Like most things, air is made up of tiny particles called molecules. When air is heated, its molecules move more quickly and spread out so a given amount of air takes up more space. If the air is contained so it cannot expand, its pressure increases instead.

When air is cooled, its molecules slow down and move nearer to each other. Its pressure then decreases.

Rising air (pages 8-9)

Because air molecules spread out when heated, a certain volume of hot air is lighter than the same volume of cold air. This makes the hot air rise, and float above the cold air.

Wind (pages 10-11)

The wind frequently changes its direction and speed. The faster a wind moves, the more strongly its effects are felt.

Air power (pages 12-13)

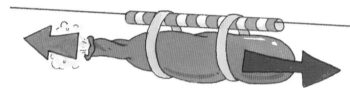

The air inside the rocket balloon is under greater pressure than the air outside. When the peg is taken off, the pressurized air rushes out of the balloon. Newton's third scientific law states that to every action there is an equal and opposite reaction. The balloon obeys this law by moving in the opposite direction to the escaping air.

Moving through air (pages 14-15)

When things move through air, they have to overcome the air pressure rushing against them. This slowing-down effect of the air is called air resistance. Some shapes encounter more air resistance than others.

Trapped air pushes hard against a parachute.

A parachute is shaped so it can use air resistance as a 'brake' to slow down a fall. Weight can help to overcome air resistance so when heavier toys are attached to the model parachute they fall faster than light toys.

Flying (pages 16-17)

The fast-flowing air above a plane's wing is at a lower pressure than the slower-moving air beneath. The difference in pressure results in a 'lift' which is strong enough to support the weight of the plane.

Breathing (pages 18-19)

When air is taken into your lungs, some of the oxygen dissolves into your bloodstream. The blood carries oxygen to every cell in your body and takes carbon dioxide gas (a waste-product of the cells) back to the lungs. The carbon dioxide is exhaled together with the parts of the air, such as nitrogen gas, that the body cannot use.

Carbon dioxide goes in.

Oxygen goes out.

Sound (pages 20-21)

Sound is a form of traveling energy produced when an object vibrates. The vibrations travel through the air and make your eardrum begin to vibrate. Your nervous system registers these vibrations as sound.

Index

American edition 1991.

First published in 1991 by Usborne Publishing Ltd, Usborne House, 83-85 Saffron Hill London EC1N 8RT, England.Copyright © 1991 Usborne Publishing Ltd www.usborne.com